FLOWERS

EMBROIDERED TREASURES

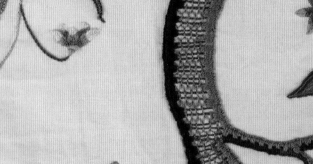
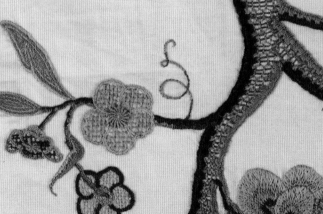

First published in 2018

Search Press Limited
Wellwood, North Farm Road,
Tunbridge Wells, Kent TN2 3DR

ISBN: 978-1-78221-131-0

3361408075744S

Printed in China through Asia Pacific Offset

Photographs
Cover image: Hot iron transfer panel, page 122.
Previous page: Crewelwork sampler, page 33.
Right: Oya, page 43.
Opposite: Embroidery on leather, page 63.

ACKNOWLEDGEMENTS

My thanks go to:
Pat Tempest, from the Embroiderers' Guild, and
Roz Dace, consultant editor for Search Press, who
originally thought of these books;
Catherine Sprowl, my assistant Collection Manager,
for her unfailing support;
and Marion Brookes from Woking Evening Branch of
the Embroiderers' Guild for her encouragement.

DEDICATION
To my mother, Joyce Cooper

EMBROIDERED TREASURES
FLOWERS

Exquisite Needlework of the Embroiderers' Guild Collection

DR ANNETTE COLLINGE

SEARCH PRESS

CONTENTS

HISTORY OF THE EG
AND ITS COLLECTION

Embroiderers' Guild Patron: HRH The Duchess of Gloucester

The Embroiderers' Guild was formed in 1906 from the desire of a small group of enthusiasts to improve the quality of design and technique among embroiderers who, they felt, had become slaves to the published chart and printed canvas, and rarely attempted their own unique designs.

This group of 16 women were graduates from the Royal School of Art Needlework, which later became the Royal School of Needlework. The catchy title they came up with was The Society of Certificated Embroideresses of the Royal School of Art Needlework, but this was changed after the First World War to the Embroiderers' Guild, a much friendlier title.

The Embroiderers' Guild Collection is nearly as old as the Embroiderers' Guild itself. Our first president was Louisa Pesel, who was elected after the First World War and it was due to her involvement with the Women's Institute (WI) that the seeds of the Collection were sown. At a lecture she gave at a WI conference, people enquired if the examples of embroidery she had brought along could be borrowed.

Before long, a committee was in place at the Embroiderers' Guild headquarters to deal with 'model' or example boxes of embroideries and

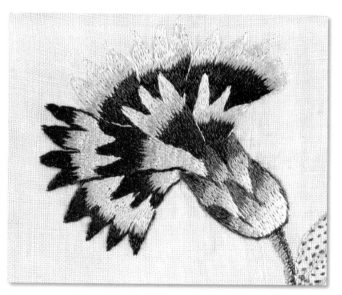

their distribution to the members on a regular basis, to improve their knowledge of design and technique. Members were allowed to handle the embroideries and encouraged to examine them closely. This resulted in an ongoing need to launder, repair and replace the existing embroideries.

Members made and donated embroideries to the model boxes and these continue today in the form of folios, which are available for members to borrow; the contents cover many aspects of embroidery. The original model boxes are thought to have been small boxes rather like laundry boxes, fastened with a leather strap. Current folios are enclosed in bright yellow folders. They now represent our educational resource but are not part of the Embroiderers' Guild Collection.

The Permanent Collection started as a result of donations that were too large or valuable to be put in a model box. Queen Mary donated large hangings and costume pieces and Lady Mary Cayley donated valuable 17th century pieces. Travellers and scholars also donated their collections of international embroideries and so the Embroiderers' Guild Permanent Collection was formed.

The Collection developed slowly and it was not until 1971 that the first catalogue was produced, when the number of embroideries listed was 114. There are now nearly 6,000 beautiful embroidered pieces in the Embroiderers' Guild Collection.

The Collection has seen a number of homes in London, including Grosvenor Street and its second most well-known home, Wimpole Street. When the lease ran out at Wimpole Street, the Collection had a number of temporary homes, including Greycoat Place where, it is said, the Collection was stored above a chip shop.

The most famous address was an apartment at Hampton Court Palace, where the Collection was stored to museum standards for the first time. This was followed by EG House in Walton-upon-Thames and currently the Collection is housed at Bucks County Museum Resource Centre near Aylesbury, UK.

Members have always been very protective of their Collection and small hitches such as world wars have not posed a problem, as members simply took the Collection home with them to be looked after until conditions improved.

British embroideries form the main body of the Collection, with the earliest pieces from the 16th century. Sadly, there are only a few of these, but samples increase in numbers through each century to the present day. The earliest pieces in the Collection are not embroideries, but Coptic weavings, which were preserved in dry sandy graves dating back to the 6th to 10th centuries.

The 20th century sees the largest number of pieces in the Collection, ranging from domestic embroideries and pictures, often made from hot iron transfer designs, to the inception of textile art in the mid to late part of the century, when the Embroiderers' Guild specifically collected contemporary embroidery and work by textile artists.

Various Embroiderers' Guild members in the past were travellers and scholars and, through their donations, we have extensive numbers of embroideries from China, India, Turkey, Greece and Eastern Europe. Less well represented are Japan, Scandinavia and the Americas.

Originally, the Collection was solely for the membership and this is still the case today. Membership of the Embroiderers' Guild entitles members to see and photograph any piece from the Collection. Travelling exhibitions enable us to reach members further afield. Smaller pieces are distributed among the folios and these are constantly added to by donations and bequests.

We continue to have very supportive members working today, who have donated their artwork to the Collection. These pieces are supplemented by the purchase of contemporary textile art, keeping the Collection up to date and relevant to the present day.

Dr Annette Collinge

INTRODUCTION

Flowers were certainly in existence when humans first used a needle and thread for decorative rather than functional purposes, but their importance in embroidery only came about in the 16th century when ladies, appreciating the beauty and symbolism of flowers, used floral images to decorate costume and furnishings.

From medieval times up to the 14th century very few flowers can be found, although scrolling stems and leaves do appear. Vines, oak and ivy foliage are seen. Where flowers are depicted, they are stylised. Most embroidery of that period was ecclesiastical in nature and one flower that did appear, albeit in stylised form, was the Madonna lily.

By the 15th century, flowers in embroidery were more realistic. Embroidered flower designs were cut out and applied to silk and velvet fabrics, often edged with couched, silver gilt thread. Tudor roses and lilies appeared. During Elizabethan times, when pattern books and herbals were available for designs, roses, violas, honeysuckle (eglantine), carnations (gillyflowers) and daffodils appeared.

In the late 16th century, Spanish blackwork became popular and it is from this period and style of embroidery that the earliest depiction of flowers can be found in the Embroiderers' Guild Collection. This technique is said to have been introduced into the country by Catherine of Aragon, the first wife of Henry VIII.

In the 17th century, elaborate bouquets of flowers in urns came to the fore, probably influenced by Dutch floral paintings of that time, and also crewel embroidery in wool, often in tones of just a few colours. During the 18th century, professional embroiderers and women with the time and money to spend on materials embroidered using designs made by professional pattern drawers. Techniques were varied and flowers were the image of choice. Costume of all kind was elaborately decorated with floral forms.

Ribbon embroidery, chenille threads and aerophane (a fine silk, crepe chiffon) introduced the even more unusual techniques of the 19th century when fish bones and scales, animal hair and straw provided interest to the Victorian lady's embroidery.

The 20th century saw the formation of the Embroiderers' Guild and a return to good design and technique. Flowers were beautifully represented. In the 1980s, the popularity of creative embroidery and textile art led to an explosion of modern techniques using paint, plastics and synthetic fabrics and threads. The flower once again became stylised and abstract in many artists' work, but at the same time, beautiful, traditional, embroidered flowers are being stitched today with the same precision as our ancestors used.

EMBROIDERY IN MONOCHROME:
BLACKWORK AND WHITEWORK

This chapter represents a tiny fraction of the embroideries in the Embroiderers' Guild Collection that can be described as monochrome, which means embroidery in a single colour on a background fabric.

Other colours can be found, including blue, red and green, often in the embroideries of Eastern Europe. Blackwork using traditional stitches but with coloured threads is still made today. One example of Indian embroidery, in yellow thread, is shown later in this book on page 114.

This chapter concentrates on blackwork embroidery and the vast subject of whitework embroidery. Some of the earliest pieces in the Collection are represented by the two small blackwork motifs from the 16th century (page 14), to be compared with the 20th century blackwork (page 15). Interestingly, both include small areas of metal thread and the third example, although using blackwork stitches, is embroidered using dark brown thread.

Whitework embroidery encompasses many techniques, including lace, cutwork, pulled and drawn thread work and many others. This chapter shows that whitework embroidery can be very delicate or quite textural.

BLACKWORK MOTIFS

TECHNIQUE: hand embroidery; blackwork

DATE: late 16th century

PLACE OF ORIGIN: England

SIZE: (top) 12 x 13cm (4¾ x 5⅛in); (bottom) 8 x 8cm (3¼ x 3¼in)

Also known as Spanish blackwork, this style of embroidery is said to have been introduced in to the country by Catherine of Aragon, Henry VIII's first wife. The motifs are stylised honeysuckle and carnation flowers, stitched on linen with black silk thread. The stitches used here are Holbein stitch or double running stitch, chain stitch and filling stitches. Motifs are outlined in metal thread.

It is thought that these motifs might have been restored at some stage, as the metal threads are brighter in some areas. There is also an area where netting has been applied to help protect the embroidery. In the 16th century, real gold and silver was used to make threads by wrapping very thin, drawn-out metal round a silk core.

These little motifs were probably intended as decoration on a pillow cover. Pillow covers were popular gifts in the 16th century, often stitched by young girls. These motifs have been stitched down or applied to a cotton calico fabric, which is more recent. They are very rare, as 16th century embroidery does not often survive today. In blackwork especially, the silk threads were often dyed using iron, which rotted the threads. These motifs have their own fabric storage boxes, protecting them from the light. The threads are so fragile that the pieces cannot be handled, but this is a lovely design, which could be used in many ways today. Compare these with the more contemporary blackwork opposite.

Embroiderers' Guild numbers: (top) EG207; (bottom) EG206

BLACKWORK WITH METAL THREAD

TECHNIQUE: hand embroidery; blackwork with metal thread

DATE: late 20th century

PLACE OF ORIGIN: England

SIZE: 33.5 x 25.5cm (13¼ x 10in)

This is blackwork brought into the 20th century. Stitched on fine, evenweave linen, with fine, black cotton thread, the outlines are in stem stitch with traditional filling stitches and the addition of gold thread, couched down by making evenly spaced stitches over the thread. There are some areas of chain stitch in synthetic threads. Modern gold thread to be couched down is made of paper foil wrapped round a cotton or silk core.

Sprigs of primula flowers, teasel and sycamore seeds are mixed with leaves and fruit, to make a panel of outstanding workmanship. The gold thread really lifts this panel, adding an extra sparkle.

Maker: Miss Gray
Gifted by: Miss Gray
Embroiderers' Guild number: EG1297

CUSHION COVER

TECHNIQUE: hand embroidery; blackwork
DATE: early 20th century
PLACE OF ORIGIN: England
SIZE: 64 x 67cm (25¼ x 26½in)

This is a cushion cover with impact. Stitched on evenweave linen fabric using heavy twisted silk thread, the embroiderer has not used the fine blackwork techniques of the 16th century. She has considered the purpose of her embroidery and selected fabric and threads that will withstand wear, appropriate to a cushion cover.

The principle of an outlined image with filling stitches is still there, but the thread is dark brown. Not all blackwork was stitched using black threads. Red, green and blue were also used but, traditionally, blackwork is monochrome apart from the addition of metal threads. I particularly like the use of satin stitch as an outline stitch. The flowers, set in a basket, are stylised, making them more in keeping with the stylised flowers of the 16th century. In the early 20th century, embroiderers often used old textiles as inspiration for their designs.

Maker: Mrs Newall
Embroiderers' Guild number: EG2079

CHIKAN EMBROIDERY

TECHNIQUE: whitework,
Chikan embroidery

DATE: 20th century

PLACE OF ORIGIN: India (Lucknow)

SIZE: 45cm (17¾in) in diameter

Made in the form of a 12-pointed star, this embroidery is typical of Chikan embroidery, which is white thread worked on white fabric. It originates from Lucknow in India, where it is said to have been introduced by the wife of a Mughal emperor. It is a traditional technique dating from the 3rd century.

Light fabrics such as muslin, silk and cotton are used, with backstitch and chain stitch for the embroidery. Designs are block printed on to the fabric and the finished embroidery is washed to remove traces of the design. The design of this piece is stylised flowers within a tangle of stems and buds or berries.

It might have been a cover or perhaps a table centrepiece. More recently, Chikan embroidery is found on garments. Today the markets of Lucknow abound with clothing of all sorts embellished with Chikan embroidery, often using coloured threads and rather less delightful than this beautiful piece.

Embroiderers' Guild number: EG1773

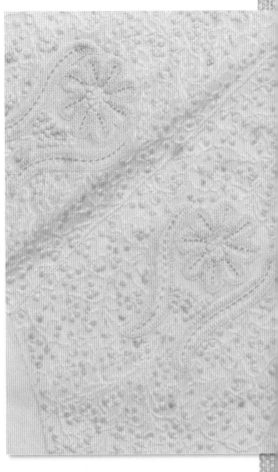

WHITEWORK SACHET

TECHNIQUE: whitework

DATE: 19th century

PLACE OF ORIGIN: Great Britain

SIZE: 36.5 x 46cm (14½ x 18in)

I love this piece for its lustrous silk threads and hand embroidery on a matt cotton background. The flowers are outlined in buttonhole stitch and filled with seeding stitch. The ferns and smaller flowers are worked in satin stitch. Note the tiny butterfly.

It is a nightdress case in a simple sachet style and would look as good on a modern bed as it would have done in the 19th century.

Embroiderers' Guild number: EG2470

SAMPLER MAT

TECHNIQUE: whitework
DATE: early 20th century
PLACE OF ORIGIN: Great Britain
SIZE: 39 x 37cm (15³⁄₈ x 14½in)

This monogrammed linen mat might be described as a sampler, as a number of different techniques have been used. They include drawn thread and pulled work, where threads are removed from the fabric and weaving with a needle, and fine thread is then used to create a design on the remaining threads.

The rose petals show different filling stitches and are outlined in satin stitch. There is an interesting monogram of intertwined letters, with a griffon on the top. The flowers depicted are roses, violets, thistles and foxgloves.

Gifted by: Lady Lawrence
Embroiderers' Guild number: EG1738

MOUNTMELLICK MAT

TECHNIQUE: Mountmellick work
DATE: late 19th century
PLACE OF ORIGIN: Ireland
SIZE: 56 x 33cm (22 x 13in)

We started this chapter with early, very fine blackwork and now we finish with more recent chunky whitework from Ireland. Mountmellick embroidery is a whitework technique, using white cotton thread on white cotton fabric.

Mountmellick embroidery was introduced after the Irish potato famine, which started in the mid 19th century. Potato blight attacked the staple crop and income for the people was critically reduced. Needlework and craft schemes were set up by groups of ladies in an attempt to provide income for poverty-stricken women.

It was developed in the late 19th century in the town of Mountmellick, Ireland, and early examples featured the plants found around the town. Blackberries, ferns, dog roses, shamrocks and acorns are often portrayed. In this early example we can see pansies and roses. The knitted fringe and embroidery are typical of Mountmellick work.

Embroiderers' Guild number: not yet accessioned

EMBROIDERY ON
EVENWEAVE BACKGROUNDS

An evenweave background can be anything from a delicate muslin through to a coarse canvas and includes net. In most cases, the embroidery is executed by counting threads in the ground fabric, most noticeably illustrated by the examples in this chapter of Berlin work and petit point. But pattern darning is another technique where the holes in the net are counted.

Beadwork is included in this chapter, although it is the way the beads are positioned that is even, rather than the ground fabric.

BEADWORK PANELS

TECHNIQUE: beadwork

DATE: 17th century

PLACE OF ORIGIN: Great Britain

SIZE (top panel) 27.5 x 21cm
(10¾ x 8¼in); (bottom panels)
24 x 10cm (9½ x 4in)

These three panels are worked with beads and stumpwork. They are showing their age, but nonetheless, they are rare and very beautiful. The glass beads have retained their lustre.

The panels are thought to be the top and two sides of a box, which might have been made to contain an Elizabethan gentleman's ruff or collar. The original fabric is linen, but these panels were glued onto cardboard relatively recently, which is a terrible thing to do to historic textiles.

The flowers are entirely depicted in coloured glass beads on a background of white beads. The yellow bowl-like flower at the bottom left of the scene is reminiscent of a waterlily. We have no provenance for this piece, but we do know it was part of the Collection before 1987. I wonder why the box was never finished.

Embroiderers' Guild number: T329

KNITTED BEADWORK BAG

TECHNIQUE: knitted beadwork
DATE: early 20th century
PLACE OF ORIGIN: Europe
SIZE: 37 x 24cm (14½ x 9½in)

This beautiful bag has been knitted with a bead added to the design of stylised flowers with every stitch. The thread is very fine and the cast-on edges are visible at the base of the bag. This bag was worked on very fine knitting needles.

The well-chosen metal frame adds lustre to the already lustrous beads. The flowers are fanciful rather than accurate representations of species, but I feel the exuberance of the design makes up for that. How lovely and shimmery this bag would look by candlelight. Later in the book, we will see an exquisite bag of ribbonwork (see page 49).

Purchased from an antiques shop in Petersfield, Hampshire, UK
Embroiderers' Guild number: EG2003.5

BEADED BAGS

TECHNIQUE: beadwork

DATE: (top) mid 19th century;
(bottom) late 19th century

PLACE OF ORIGIN: Great Britain

SIZE: (top) 22 x 14.5cm (8¾ x 5¾in);
(bottom) 20 x 7cm (8 x 2¾in)

These bags are very beautiful examples of beadwork. The top example is knitted and has a leather lining and the red bag below is a lovely little miser's purse, where the beads are stitched onto a red fabric. The flowers depicted on the top bag are roses, daffodils and marigolds, in a riot of colour and floral splendour.

Miser's purses originated in the late 18th century and were popular up to the early 1900s. They were used by both women and men and were a very secure way of keeping coins or precious objects safe.

The purses are tube-like with a long slit and two metal rings held tightly round the middle. By moving one or other of the rings, coins or jewellery could be dropped in either end of the purse and by returning the ring to its original position were safely sealed.

The little beads stitched to this purse dictate the style of the flowers. There are tiny daisies decorating the edges, where a gold bead is surrounded by a single circle of white beads. The flowers at the centre of each end are more elaborate. On this purse, the shimmer is made mainly by the gold beads, the others being less reflective.

Flower detail from miser's purse, below

Miser's bag gifted by: Miss K. Aldworth
Embroiderers' Guild number: (top)
EG2731; (bottom) EG4675

24

BEADED TEA COSY

TECHNIQUE: Berlin work, beaded
DATE: late 19th century
PLACE OF ORIGIN: Great Britain
SIZE: 28 x 44cm (11 x 17¼in)

This is a Berlin work tea cosy. Berlin wool work is a style of embroidery similar to today's needlepoint and was typically worked in wool yarn on canvas.

It was worked from a chart where the squares were coloured in, so that the embroiderer could follow it easily. Each square represented a stitch. These charts originated in Berlin, hence the name.

The tea cosy is stitched in tent stitch, with grisaille beads forming the flowers. Grisaille beadwork was stitched using white, clear, grey and black beads against a background of brilliant red or blue. Note the intense colours of this piece. Up until the mid 19th century, dyes used to colour fabrics were natural dyes, but by the time of Berlin wool work, aniline (synthetic) dyes had been introduced and a whole new world of colour was opened up to the embroiderer.

Embroiderers' Guild number: EG5883

DAFFODIL TRAY CLOTH

TECHNIQUE: pattern darning on net

DATE: 20th century (1934–1937)

PLACE OF ORIGIN: India (Tamil Nadu, Vellore)

SIZE: 38 x 25cm (15 x 10in)

This is a tray cloth featuring a design of daffodils, darned directly onto very fine, white, machine-made net and using cotton thread.

Darning is achieved with a needle and thread where the needle is pushed in and out of the net, making lines of thread according to the design. It is very delicate for a tray cloth and was gifted to the Embroiderers' Guild with a tea cosy of a similar design and technique.

Vellore is in the area of Tamil Nadu in India. A Christian medical college and hospital was founded in 1900 by an American woman from a family of missionaries, originally living in India. This may explain why the design and style of the piece is not typical of Indian designs.

Maker: Vellore American Mission, India
Embroiderers' Guild number: EG1982.55.2

PETIT POINT BAGS

TECHNIQUE: petit point

DATE: (top) 19th century; (bottom) early 20th century

PLACE OF ORIGIN: Great Britain

SIZE: (top) 14 x 16.5cm (5½ x 6½in);
(bottom) 10 x 12cm (4 x 4¾in)

These exquisite little purses are stitched using the technique called petit point, which means little stitches. Fine cotton threads are used on very fine canvas in tent stitch. Notice how only the floral design is covered in stitches, the rest of the canvas being left blank.

There are roses, morning glories and primulas in the design, together with forget-me-nots. The design would have been worked from a chart. The donor of these bags gave a great number of embroideries to the collection in the early 20th century.

Gifted by: Miss Hester Clough
Hester Clough, who lived in Hampshire, UK, was a significant donor to the Embroiderers' Guild Collection.
Embroiderers' Guild numbers: (bottom) EG1987.36;
(top) EG1987.37

Flower detail from bag, above

CANVAS WORK FRAGMENT

TECHNIQUE: canvas work; tent stitch

DATE: 17th century (1670)

PLACE OF ORIGIN: Great Britain

SIZE: 33.5 x 16cm (13 x 6¼in)

We find ourselves back in the 17th century for this very rare fragment of tent stitch on canvas. The background is stitched in wool thread and the floral design is in silk. The flower is a rose.

This is probably a fragment from furnishings – perhaps a chair cover. It is exciting to imagine how the whole piece would have looked with the dark green background and swirling, slightly shimmery flowers and leaves. How lovely it would have been to see it by candlelight.

Gifted by: Miss K. Paget

This fragment can be found in one of our folios, as part of our educational resource.

CORNUCOPIA DARNING SAMPLER

TECHNIQUE: pattern darning
DATE: late 18th century
PLACE OF ORIGIN: Great Britain
SIZE: 16 x 77cm (6¼ x 30in)

This is a darning sampler, which uses a similar technique to the daffodil tray cloth on page 26. A very fine linen ground is embroidered with silk threads, showing how effective pattern darning is as a technique on evenweave fabric. Outlines have been stitched in stem and buttonhole stitch. Notice how the darned sections on the border are divided by a narrow band of pulled work. Notice also the initials AT on the bottom of the sampler.

The design is a cornucopia of flowers and leaves surrounded with leaf shapes. Some of us remember darning socks and learned the technique at home or school. This intricate and colourful sampler utilises the same technique and shows just how beautiful the rather mundane darning can be.

Darning samplers had become popular before the 18th century, at a time when mass production was not yet thought of. Making clothes last longer by employing fine darning repairs was a very useful skill and needlewomen made samplers in different colours and darning patterns to show off their needlework accomplishments.

Embroiderers' Guild number: EG1991

SAMPLERS
AND SAMPLES

Traditionally, a sampler is an embroidery designed to show the expertise of the embroiderer and to keep as a reference of techniques and designs.

Early samplers worked by young girls were part of their educational progress in needlework and they would progress from samplers to more ambitious projects.

From the mid 20th century, the term sampler became popular to describe pictorial embroideries in which many stitches were used, as in the crewelwork sampler (see page 33), designed as a fire screen, but displaying as many stitches as the embroiderer could fit in. The little fabric book on page 35 is not a sampler in the true sense, but is a collection of samples, looking back to the early samplers used as a reference of designs.

CHILD'S SAMPLER

TECHNIQUE: hand embroidery
DATE: 17th century (1657)
PLACE OF ORIGIN: Great Britain
SIZE: 90 x 26cm (35½ x 10¼in)

The legend on this embroidered sampler reads: 'Mary Powell wrought this sampler being ten years old 1657'. That makes it nearly 360 years old.

This sampler would have been part of Mary's education in needlework. It would have been made as a reference of designs, which she might use in later work and a showcase of her skills as she practised new techniques and stitches.

In 17th century embroidery, motifs and designs were often copied from other embroideries or from printed patterns, which were available for purchase. The flowers are stylised and the number of stitches used is impressive. In the blue flowers, every petal is a different stitch. The background is natural linen and the threads are silk. I am amazed at the skill shown in this sampler, made by such a young needlewoman.

Maker: Mary Powell (aged 10 years)
Gifted by: Miss Hester Clough
Embroiderers' Guild number:
EG1987.23

CREWELWORK SAMPLER

TECHNIQUE: crewelwork

DATE: 20th century (1934)

PLACE OF ORIGIN: Great Britain

SIZE: 97.5 x 58.5cm (38³/₈ x 23in)

In the 20th century, the term sampler was used less formally than in the 17th century example opposite. Samplers were often pictorial with different stitches used for different parts of the design.

This sampler is an example of this. It is a Jacobean-style design in crewelwork of a tree of life with stylised flowers. It is made as a sampler, to try out different stitches. The origin of the word 'crewel' is not known, but the technique was in use in the 17th century. Both embroiderers have used different stitches in their samplers. Mary Powell's technique is counted thread embroidery and, 300 years later, Mary Clarke's technique is free embroidery.

What is especially nice about this piece is that Mary has embroidered her name and the date she stitched it – something that did not always happen in the 20th century. The background is linen and the thread used is wool. Mary says of it: 'It was to be a fire screen but had been tucked away in a drawer. I tried to use as many stitches as possible.'

Maker: Mary Clarke (while a student at Harrogate College of Art)
Gifted by: Mary Metcalfe (née Mary Clarke)
Embroiderers' Guild number: EG5600

ROSES SAMPLER

TECHNIQUE: hand embroidery

DATE: 20th century (1947)

PLACE OF ORIGIN: Great Britain

SIZE: 39.5 x 42cm (15½ x 16½in)

This is one of a series of five embroideries in various techniques made by Nancy Kimmins, who was born in 1922. She made them while she was training at the Royal School of Needlework.

This is different from the examples we have looked at so far, being a sampler of just one technique, to show the expertise of the embroiderer in that technique. Nancy went on to be a highly regarded tutor, embroiderer and member of the Embroiderers' Guild.

The fabric is a natural, evenweave linen stitched with wool threads. Stitches used are long and short stitch, and satin stitch, and the flowers are undoubtedly roses.

Maker: Nancy Kimmins (while at the Royal School of Needlework)
Gifted by: Nancy Kimmins
Embroiderers' Guild number: EG1984.10.2

BOOK OF SAMPLES

TECHNIQUE: hand embroidery
DATE: mid 20th century
PLACE OF ORIGIN: Great Britain
SIZE: each page is 17.5 x 14.5cm
(7 x 5¾in)

This is a further example of a sampler made in the 20th century and represents another way of working a sampler with ideas for future work. It is a handmade fabric book of samples of many techniques, with the maker's name embroidered on the front. Some of the 12 pages are canvas, for counted thread techniques. Berlin work and needle lace are featured, but these flowers are embroidered on cotton calico with stranded cotton thread.

The maker used lovely vibrant colours and it is beautifully stitched in long and short stitch, French knots and satin stitch – such a lovely way to create a stitch sampler.

Maker: Beatrice M. McCarthy Main
Gifted by: her daughter, Mrs C. Elphick
Embroiderers' Guild number: EG3943

Below: This is the reverse of a page above (middle, right) to show how neat the reverse of the work is.

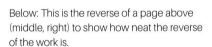

Detail, middle left

Detail, top

FLORAL SAMPLER

TECHNIQUE: silk shading and metal thread embroidery, including Or Nué

DATE: 20th century (1940)

PLACE OF ORIGIN: Great Britain

SIZE: 47 x 51cm (18½ x 20in)

This spectacularly beautiful work was achieved by a student at the Royal School of Needlework. Sadly, we do not know her name, but we do know that all apprentices and students followed a strict course with a graded series of samplers all representing a particular technique.

We have two complete named sets of Royal School of Needlework samplers in the Embroiderers' Guild Collection. The fabric is linen twill, stitched with silk thread and metal threads in a number of stitches including long and short, laid work, couching and Or Nué. See page 70 for another example of Or Nué work.

The technique of Or Nué is particularly beautiful. Metal threads are laid down on a background fabric in parallel lines. These are then stitched over, using one or more colours to create an image upon the metal thread background. The flowers are very realistic, including a Tudor rose, a lily and a carnation. Taking a flower and portraying it accurately in thread is a splendid achievement for all embroiderers.

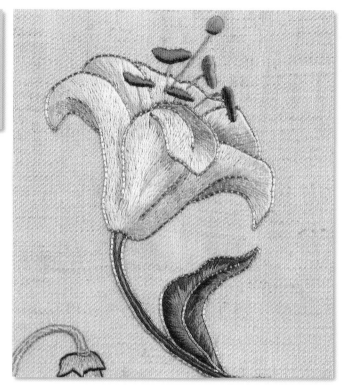

Maker: Royal School of Needlework student

Embroiderers' Guild number: EG1985.2

This sampler is on indefinite loan to the Royal School of Needlework.

VERSE SAMPLER

TECHNIQUE: hand embroidery

DATE: 19th century (1824)

PLACE OF ORIGIN: Great Britain

SIZE: 44.5 x 34.5cm (17½ x 13½in)

Elisabeth Barratt does not give us her age, but her sampler was finished on October 30th 1824. We have samplers of this type in the Embroiderers' Guild collection from embroiderers aged from 6 years to 16 years. I would suggest Elisabeth was only 10 or 12 years old.

Elisabeth's sampler is a verse sampler stitched on evenweave linen in cross, stem, long and short and satin stitch, using cotton thread. There are roses, primroses and carnations on this sampler, the flowers being more realistic than on the very early example by Mary Powell (see page 32).

I find these early samplers worked by children so inspiring and a design that can be achieved today. Today's samplers are often stitched entirely in cross stitch, but I prefer the variety of stitches seen here.

Maker: Elisabeth Barratt

Gifted by: Needlework Development Scheme in 1962

Embroiderers' Guild number: EG1472

This sampler is on indefinite loan to the University of Edinburgh.

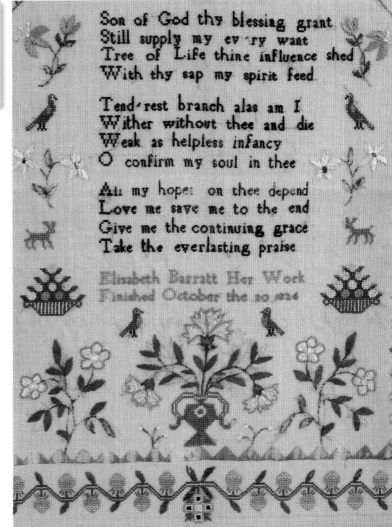

Son of God thy blessing grant
Still supply my ev'ry want
Tree of Life thine influence shed
With thy sap my spirit feed

Tend'rest branch alas am I
Wither without thee and die
Weak as helpless infancy
O confirm my soul in thee

All my hopes on thee depend
Love me save me to the end
Give me the continuing grace
Take the everlasting praise

Elisabeth Barratt Her Work
Finished October the 30 1824

NEEDLE LACE

This chapter concentrates on lace and lace-like effects created by needle and thread, often on a framework of threads or wire, to create a raised effect in embroidery.

It includes some of our earliest embroideries from the 17th century, to be compared with the contemporary 3D embroidery on page 81. A whitework sampler from the 17th century shows delicate needle lace flowers in white threads (see page 42), which should be compared with the 20th century brightly coloured oyas from Turkey on page 43. Needle lace is often found on garments and many examples originate from Italy.

COIF PANEL

TECHNIQUE: needle lace
DATE: early 17th century
PLACE OF ORIGIN: Great Britain
SIZE: 25.5 x 43cm (10 x 17in)

This is a coif or lady's headpiece. Compare it to the late 16th century blackwork motifs at the beginning of this book, a technique that continued into the 17th century when this coif was made.

Notice the colours in this coif and the more realistic flowers crowded onto the linen ground. Threads are silk and silver gilt with spangles and metal plate. Here is the complicated plaited braid stitch, chain stitches and, especially, needle lace, which is made using needle and thread over a framework of threads to create a filling of stitches that are not attached to the background fabric.

This piece is in beautiful condition and very rare. It lives protected from light in a specially made calico box.

Gifted by: Lady Mary Cayley, one of the first donors of important pieces to the Embroiderers' Guild Collection
Embroiderers' Guild number: EG161

PEA POD PANEL

TECHNIQUE: needle lace
DATE: early 17th century
PLACE OF ORIGIN: Great Britain
SIZE: 22.5 x 42.5cm (8⅞ x 16¾in)

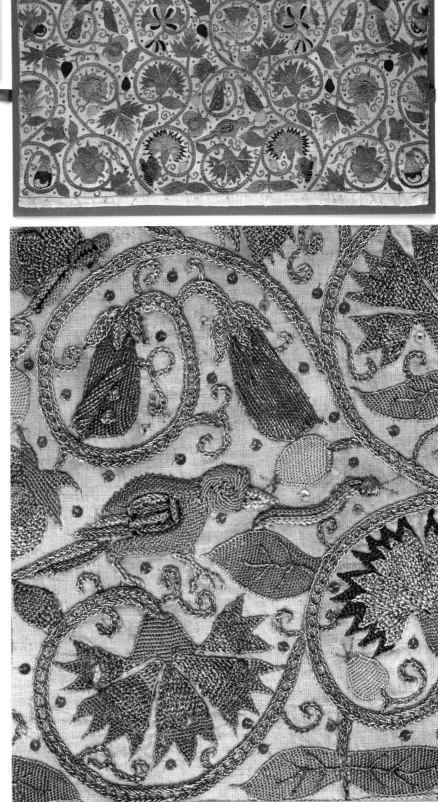

Always known as the pea pod panel, this astounding example of 17th century embroidery features needle lace pea pods, which peel back to reveal golden peas. Similar in style and execution to the earlier coif opposite, this too may be a coif panel.

Some of the flowers are stitched in needle lace over padding, raising them above the surface. This piece is also kept in a calico box to exclude light. It is a privilege of membership of the Embroiderers' Guild that members may see these pieces.

The Needlework Development Scheme was started in 1934 by Scottish Art Colleges to encourage education in needlework and embroidery. Pieces (usually domestic) were made for the scheme, but historic and international pieces were also donated. This is one of the historic pieces. When the Scheme closed in 1960, the collection was distributed among Scottish colleges, the Victoria and Albert Museum and the Embroiderers' Guild.

Gifted by: Needlework Development Scheme in 1962
Embroiderers' Guild number: EG1982.79

WHITEWORK SAMPLER

TECHNIQUE: needle lace
DATE: late 17th century
PLACE OF ORIGIN: Great Britain
SIZE: 49.5 x 16.5cm (19½ x 16½in)

We have seen blackwork from the late 16th century and now, in the late 17th century, we have whitework on a sampler showing many techniques, including needle lace. The luscious rose and iris are in detached buttonhole stitch on a framework of laid threads.

In this technique, the needle does not go through the background fabric, but tiny, interlinking stitches are made within the framework, resulting in a raised flower. White linen threads have been used on a white linen ground fabric.

This sampler shows the great skills achieved by embroiderers of the 17th century. It arrived at the Embroiderers' Guild as a donation with several 17th century samplers by Deborah Palmer, assumed to be a child; this piece, however, might have been professionally made.

Embroiderers' Guild number: EG4019

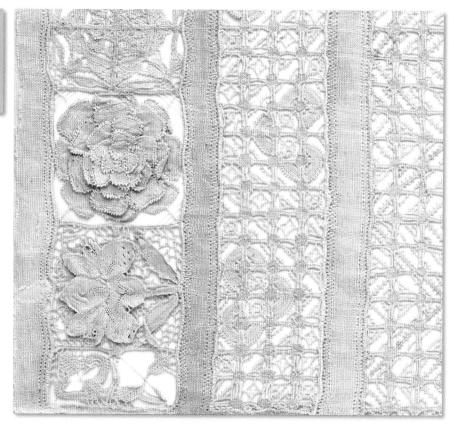

OYAS

TECHNIQUE: needle lace
DATE: 20th century
PLACE OF ORIGIN: Turkey, Greece, Greek Islands
SIZE: individual flowers: 1.5–3cm (⅝–1¼in)

These lovely lengths of individual needle lace flowers are called oyas or bebilla and they are characteristic of Greece and Turkey. They are made from needle lace and used as an edging round scarves and shawls.

The flowers and other designs are important as they reveal the status of the wearer. I love the colourful flowers, but it is possible that the black ones are worn for mourning as they are quite sombre compared to the others.

Gifted by: Miss H. E. Ionides in 1962

Miss Ionides was a generous donor of Greek and Turkish embroideries to the Embroiderers' Guild Collection.

Embroiderers' Guild number: (bottom) EG2596; top piece is not yet accessioned

NEEDLE LACE CUFF

TECHNIQUE: needle lace
DATE: 17ᵗʰ century (1630)
PLACE OF ORIGIN: Great Britain
SIZE: 41 x 20cm (16¹⁄₈ x 8in)

How lovely to imagine this cuff being worn in 1630. It is typical of the English needle lace of this period.

The fabric is fine linen and the needle lace flowers are built up on a grid of laid and plaited threads. This technique makes the design quite geometric, but notice how it has been softened by the scallops of needle lace at the edge.

Gifted by: Lady Lawrence
Embroiderers' Guild number: EGL166

RETICELLA MATS

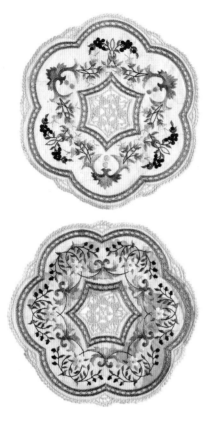
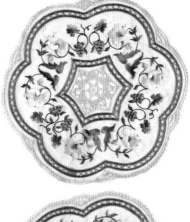

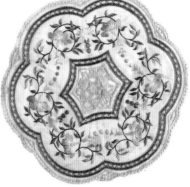

TECHNIQUE: hand embroidery; reticella
DATE: early 20th century
PLACE OF ORIGIN: Italy
SIZE: 16cm (6¼in) in diameter

Silk and couched metal threads with a centre of reticella lace make up the embroidery on these six little mats, which probably come from Italy. Reticella is needle lace dating from the 15th century. Threads are withdrawn from a linen background to make a grid on which the fabric is stitched with a needle and thread. It has a characteristic geometric design. Each mat has a different floral design including strawberries, daffodils and roses.

Gifted by: Miss Hester Clough
Embroiderers' Guild number: (top left) 1987.105.5; (top middle) 1987.105.3; (top right) 1987.105.2; (bottom left) 1987.105.1; (bottom middle) 1987.105.6; (bottom right) 1987.105.4

APPLIED
MATERIALS

In this chapter we look at techniques where fabric is used to convey a design onto other fabrics, by cutting out shapes in fabric and stitching them to a background; and also techniques where objects are attached to fabric by stitching, to create a design or pattern, or to add meaning to a contemporary artwork. Ribbonwork is another applied technique, which involves manipulation of the ribbons before stitching them in place. We also look at the addition of beads, buttons and sequins and, from India, shisha mirrors.

SILK RIBBON FOOT COVER

TECHNIQUE: ribbonwork
DATE: 19th–20th century (1890–1930)
PLACE OF ORIGIN: Great Britain
SIZE: 129 x 78cm (50¾ x 30¾in)

Ribbon embroidery was very popular in the late 19th century and was used to decorate clothing and accessories. Ribbons were made commercially in England and France, in a wide range of widths and colours to accommodate embroidery on tiny pincushions and large pieces such as this cover.

The technique of ribbon embroidery was very effective and quick and easy to do. Ribbons were manipulated and sewn in place. The final result was not washable, so ribbons were used to decorate bags, purses and garments such as evening wear, which were unlikely to require laundering.

This is a unique cover; pink silk fabric is decorated with silk ribbons and backed with blue silk. The ribbons are manipulated and sewn down to make flowers. Coiled metal threads have been used to make the centres of the flowers. It is a very feminine piece, suitable for a lady's boudoir and has an amazing history, as it was once used by Queen Mary to cover her feet as she reclined on a chaise longue. I like to think the chaise longue was also pink.

Although it is not thought that Queen Mary made this piece, she was a talented needlewoman and was patron of the Embroiderers' Guild from before 1932 until her death in 1953. Records do not say specifically when this piece was made. It seems likely that a guess was made based on Queen Mary's dates and the date range of popularity of the technique.

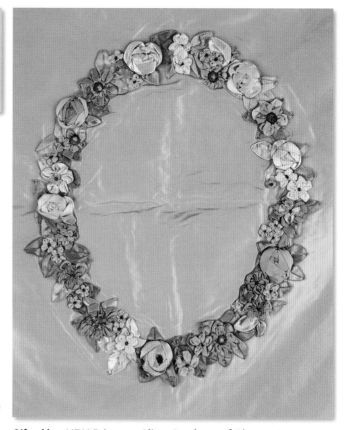

Gifted by: HRH Princess Alice, Duchess of Gloucester
Princess Alice was the daughter-in-law of Queen Mary. The Embroiderers' Guild has always had royal patronage and continues to do so. Today, the current Duchess of Gloucester is our patron.
Embroiderers' Guild number: 1987.4

RIBBONWORK BAG

TECHNIQUE: ribbonwork
DATE: late 19th century
PLACE OF ORIGIN: Great Britain
SIZE: 27.5 x 32cm (10¾ x 12½in)

This is one of my favourite pieces in the Embroiderers' Guild Collection – an exquisite evening bag, decorated with fine silk ribbon and jewels. The embroidery is in silk threads using straight stitch and French knots. The fabric is black silk with a pink silk lining and a black cord drawstring, which is rather clumsy compared to the very fine embroidery and ribbonwork (see below right).

Compare this bag to Queen Mary's foot cover (opposite) and how the width of ribbons used is appropriate to the size of the finished article.

Sadly, many of the pieces in the Collection have no provenance and the maker of this bag is not known. We can only imagine a titled lady carrying it to a ball.

Embroiderers' Guild number: EG14

APPLIED FELT TEA COSY

TECHNIQUE: felt appliqué

DATE: mid 20th century

PLACE OF ORIGIN: Great Britain

SIZE: 32 x 28cm (12½ x 11in)

A garden of flowers for an English teatime – this tea cosy is decorated with applied felt shapes, and embroidered in stranded cotton using straight stitch and French knots. The background is cotton and the lining is cotton calico.

This technique has been popular since the early 20th century. There was even a magazine dedicated to felt craft. Charts and hot iron transfers were available with the shapes numbered for ease of assembly. I love this technique; it is simple but effective and very inspirational. The felt flowers are stylised, being simple shapes cut from felt to form petals or whole flowers, which are then stitched in place to create the design.

Purchased from an internet auction site in 2014
Loaned to the Embroiderers' Guild Collection by Dr Annette Collinge

Front view

Back view

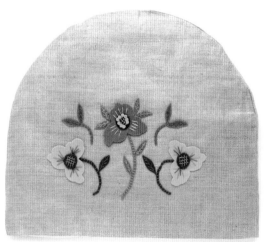

FELT SUNFLOWER PANEL

TECHNIQUE: felt appliqué
with embroidery
DATE: 20th century (1960s)
PLACE OF ORIGIN: Great Britain
SIZE: 53 x 41cm (20¾ x 16in)

This piece has great impact and is typical of the bright colours and exuberance of the 1960s. The flower is stylised, but I believe it is a sunflower. The panel has applied felt shapes embroidered with thick wool threads and some stranded cotton worked in a variety of stitches on a felt background.

This is probably an original design, as it does not have the simplicity that is shown in the tea cosy opposite.

Embroiderers' Guild number: not yet accessioned

FELT KNAPWEED PANEL

TECHNIQUE: felt work

DATE: 20th century (1970s)

PLACE OF ORIGIN: Great Britain

SIZE: 54.5 x 42cm (21½ x 16½in)

The popularity of felt embroidery had not diminished by the 1970s. This is probably another original design. Compare this panel to the tea cosy and 1960s felt panel on pages 50 and 51. There is less impact, the colours are more subdued and it might be said to be rather dark, but this is undoubtedly a knapweed (Centaurea scabiosa) and the meticulous embroidery and felt appliqué enhances the design.

The felt is applied to the dark background with surface embroidery in wool and stranded cotton threads, which have been couched down in places.

Embroiderers' Guild number: not yet accessioned

PURPLE FLOWER PANEL

TECHNIQUE: hand embroidery
DATE: 20th century (1967)
COUNTRY OF ORIGIN: Great Britain
SIZE: 25 x 20cm (9¾ x 8in)

The 1960s was a decade of colour and an 'everything goes' attitude. This purple flower on its bright pink felt background is only small, but has a big voice.

Applied fabrics, beads and sequins are enhanced with hand embroidery in stranded cotton, mostly using straight stitches. It is the simple shapes and simple stitches that give impact to this piece, and I particularly like the detail of attaching sequins using beads.

Maker: Anne Gillespie Smith
Embroiderers' Guild number: EG2337

APPLIED FABRICS PANEL

TECHNIQUE: hand embroidery

DATE: 20th century (1960s)

PLACE OF ORIGIN: Great Britain

SIZE: 48.5 x 33.5cm (19 x 13¼in)

This panel is less exuberant than the previous piece. There is no signature, but on the back, written in ink, it is stated that it was made by G. Neale at a Monday evening class with the Embroiderers' Guild.

The technique has been very carefully executed. The background is furnishing fabric, decorated with applied fabrics and padded areas. Thick and thin threads have been used with thick wool threads couched in place. Stitches include French knots, seeding stitch, chain stitch and straight stitch. The flower is very stylised, but could be a sunflower – the 1960s was the decade of flower power, after all.

Maker: G. Neale (made at an Embroiderers' Guild evening class)

Gifted by: G. Neale

Embroiderers' Guild number: EG3008

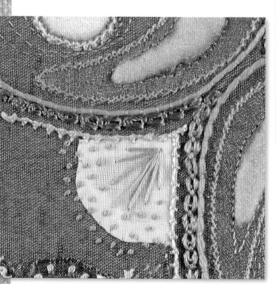

SHISHA MIRRORS BLOUSE

TECHNIQUE: shisha mirrors
DATE: 19th century
PLACE OF ORIGIN: India
SIZE: 57 x 50cm (22½ x 19¾in)

India was the first Asian country I visited and I have a special affection for its embroidery. This is a blouse front decorated with pieces of mirror called shisha, which are stitched in place with a special stitch that holds the shisha in position without the necessity of glue.

Shisha embroidery originated in the 17th century and is still found as traditional embroidery in countries of Asia. The glass was blown into large bubbles, which were then broken up into small pieces. Women used special scissors to chip the edges of the glass to make circles.

Embroiderers' Guild number: EG2293

NET APPLIQUÉ PANEL

TECHNIQUE: hand embroidery with appliqué
DATE: 20th century (1960)
PLACE OF ORIGIN: Great Britain
SIZE: 36 x 28cm (14¼ x 11in)

Here is a lovely example of 1960s work by a college student, using net appliqué and hand embroidery in stranded cotton.

Notice how the embroiderer has layered the net to create darker areas in the leaves. Satin stitch is used to outline the flowers and leaves.

Maker: Violet Geary, who was a student at Doncaster College of Art
Embroiderers' Guild number: EG2015.18

CREWELWORK SLIPS

TECHNIQUE: crewel embroidery
DATE: early 18th century
PLACE OF ORIGIN: Great Britain
SIZE: 50 x 65cm (19¾ x 25½in)

These very old flowers were rescued from an original furnishing, carefully cut out and applied to a more recent piece of linen.

In the 18th century it was common practice to embroider part of a design onto a separate piece of fabric, such as canvas. The finished designs, which were commonly flowers, were then cut out and stitched in place on other fabrics. These were called slips. These flowers and stems are stitched with wool threads on linen fabric.

Embroiderers' Guild number: EG3542

EMBROIDERY WITH
UNUSUAL MATERIALS

In this chapter we look at the strange and unusual in terms of embroidery, including straw, moose hair, fish scales and the oddly named aerophane. Many of these were popular in Victorian times.

In the 20th and 21st centuries, with the popularity of unusual materials increasing in tandem with creative embroidery, the possibilities expanded and the use of fruit and vegetable net bags (see page 65) is a typical example.

FISH SCALE EMBROIDERY

TECHNIQUE: fish scale embroidery

DATE: 19th century

PLACE OF ORIGIN: Great Britain

SIZE: 26.5 x 61cm (10½ x 24in)

This unique technique is something of a novelty. The roses are actually made by sewing down fish scales in circles and filling in the centres with floss silk threads in straight stitches.

The fish scales were first soaked in water to remove the fishy odour and two little holes were made in the base of each scale with a fine needle. The scales could then be stitched in place with a fine thread. Perch, carp and goldfish scales were used. Female fish usually have the largest scales.

The velvet fabric of this beautiful but rather strange piece sets off the fish scale roses, and the floss silk threads in chain stitch and straight stitch add to the vibrancy. We do not know what this piece is – perhaps a collar – but it wouldn't wash very well!

Gifted by: Lady Stokes
Embroiderers' Guild number: EG301

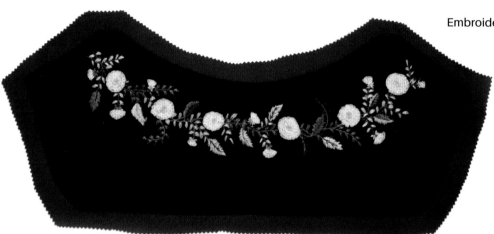

STRAW EMBROIDERY

TECHNIQUE: straw embroidery

DATE: 19th century

PLACE OF ORIGIN: Eastern Europe

SIZE: 52 x 30cm (20½ x 11¾in)

This is a very rare technique, not done today because of the patience needed to make both sides of the embroidery appear the same. It is possible that this collar – embroidered with straw on black net, with a scalloped edge – came from Russia but sadly, we have little information about it.

To use the straw for embroidery, each piece was cut along its length to make six narrow strips, which were sewn to a net background to make flowers and leaves. The straw parts are linked with perle threads woven into the net. The flowers look rather like daisies.

Victorian ladies in Great Britain liked a challenge and may well have used this technique, although they could also buy little images stamped on to straw, which they would glue to fabric. The shimmer of the gold straw against the matt black of the net makes this an eye-catching piece of work.

Embroiderers' Guild number: EGT267

EMBROIDERY ON TREE BARK

TECHNIQUE: embroidery on tree bark
DATE: 19th century (1883)
PLACE OF ORIGIN: Canada
SIZE: 4.5 x 9cm (1¾ x 3½in) in diameter

This dear little box is embroidered on birch tree bark and the thread is actually dyed moose hair. Tiny little French knots and straight stitches have been used to make flowers and leaves on the surface. Bundles of moose hairs have been couched round the top and bottom of the box with three straight stitches and, if you look carefully, you can see a diamond design woven into the three stitches.

The flowers seem quite stylised on this piece as the nuns would have brought European ideas of flowers, rather than using flowers native to Canada.

This piece is very rare as there are only three examples of embroidery on tree bark in the Collection. They are the only examples of moose hair used as a thread. All three pieces were donated by Queen Mary.

Maker: Nuns at the Ursuline Convent, Quebec, Canada
Gifted by: HM Queen Mary
Embroiderers' Guild number: EG4418

EMBROIDERY ON LEATHER

TECHNIQUE: embroidery on leather

DATE: early 20th century

PLACE OF ORIGIN: Canada

SIZE: 21 x 20cm (8¼ x 8in)

Embroidery on leather is not a rare technique, being found today on various items, particularly gloves, boots and bags. This exceptional piece is stitched with vibrant threads onto deer or moose skin. The colours are important, having special meanings to the Métis tribe of Canada.

The threads are silk. Chain stitch is used for the embroidery. Each thread starts with a stitch going through the leather, but subsequent stitches are made by catching only the surface of the leather, until the end of the thread is reached and the last stitch goes through the leather again.

This makes the finished fabric more flexible when it is worn and also makes it more waterproof because most of the stitches are on the surface of the leather and there are only holes made at the beginning and end of each thread.

Maker: West Canadian Indians from the Métis tribe

The Métis tribe are well known for their floral silk embroidery, which was taught to them by Ursuline nuns, who were embroidery teachers at the mission schools. The nuns came from Europe and this is why many of the designs, including this piece and the birch bark box opposite, show European influences. The flowers are stylised, much like the flowers on the birch bark box.

This piece was purchased by the Embroiderers' Guild for the Collection from a textile dealer in 1986.

Embroiderers' Guild number: EG1986.36

3D BOWL OF FLOWERS

TECHNIQUE: three-dimensional embroidery

DATE: late 20th century

PLACE OF ORIGIN: Great Britain

SIZE: 28cm (11in) in height

At a distance, this looks like a little bowl of flowers, but every flower, leaf and stem, and even the bowl is made of fabric and thread. It is best described as fabric and thread manipulation.

The leaves and flower petals have been cut from synthetic fabrics and the stems are wire, wrapped with cotton threads. Flower centres and some of the flowers are made from fluffy woollen threads and stitches used are a form of needle weaving, tufting and French knots.

Gifted by: a branch of the Embroiderers' Guild
Embroiderers' Guild number: not yet accessioned

EMBROIDERY USING PLASTIC NET BAGS

TECHNIQUE: appliqué with plastic net bags
DATE: mid 20th century
PLACE OF ORIGIN: Great Britain
SIZE: 46 x 26cm (18 x 10¼in)

Barbara Snook was primarily a teacher and author of embroidery books. This piece shows how original she was in her work, using cut-up plastic fruit and vegetable net bags and applying them to a fabric background with stitches in cotton thread. She has added some chain stitch and straight stitch, and incorporated some beads into the design.

I like the originality of this. It is such an inspirational piece, and makes me want to collect net bags to have a go myself. It is unique in the Embroiderers' Guild Collection, as it is the only accessioned piece made with prominent plastic net bags.

Maker: Barbara Snook (1913-1977)
Gifted by: Barbara Snook
Embroiderers' Guild number: EG2016.39

AEROPHANE EMBROIDERY

TECHNIQUE: embroidery with aerophane

DATE: early 19th century

PLACE OF ORIGIN: Great Britain

SIZE: 49 x 40cm (19¼ x 15¾in)

With a name like aerophane, you might expect a contemporary fabric, but the earliest record of aerophane is 1828. It was a fine, slightly stiff silk gauze fabric, often gathered or pleated.

The roses in this piece are made from wide aerophane ribbons, gathered and stitched down to form flowers. Entire dresses were made of aerophane and it was very popular for trimming hats. This example is stitched on black satin.

Embroiderers' Guild number: EG1990.27

3D COPPER ROSE

TECHNIQUE: three-dimensional appliqué

DATE: 20th century (1980)

PLACE OF ORIGIN: Great Britain

SIZE: 34 x 39cm (13½ x 15¼in)

This very recent donation to the Collection is a startling three-dimensional depiction of a rose. The petals are made from gold-coloured leather and the flower is embellished with metal thread and beads.

We saw embroidery on leather earlier in this book (see page 63); how different this is, with very little embroidery and using only a single colour.

Maker: Joan Hardingham

Joan was a traveller and collector of textiles who donated many beautiful pieces, including the oyas from Turkey (see page 43). We are lucky to have this sole example of her work in the Collection. She died recently, in her 90s.

Gifted by: Joan Hardingham

Embroiderers' Guild number: EG2015.16

THE USE OF
METAL THREAD

Metal thread in the Embroiderers' Guild Collection is first seen in examples from the 16th century, but the technique is much older. Many embroideries in the Collection are partly stitched with metal thread.

It is probably best known as a technique for ecclesiastical embroidery in church furnishings of many kinds. Many well-known embroiderers, past and present, are known for their church embroidery.

Costume is another category where metal thread is found worldwide and there are also ceremonial uses of the technique. Today, most metal thread work is stitched using synthetic threads, which are available for both hand and machine embroidery.

OR NUÉ PANEL

TECHNIQUE: Or Nué

DATE: 20th century (1982)

PLACE OF ORIGIN: Great Britain

SIZE: 9 x 8cm (3½ x 3¼in)

This is an outstanding technique requiring great skill and patience. Or Nué was introduced in the 15th century. Gold threads are laid down over the background fabric, very close together and parallel to each other. The design is created by the colours and spacing of fine threads, which are stitched or couched over the metal threads.

These flowers are created entirely by the threads laid over the gold threads and giving the impression of embroidery on a gold background. It is a tiny piece and one of very few examples of Or Nué in the Collection. There is another example in this book on loan to the Royal School of Needlework (see page 36).

Maker: R. Stoker

Embroiderers' Guild number: EG1985.1

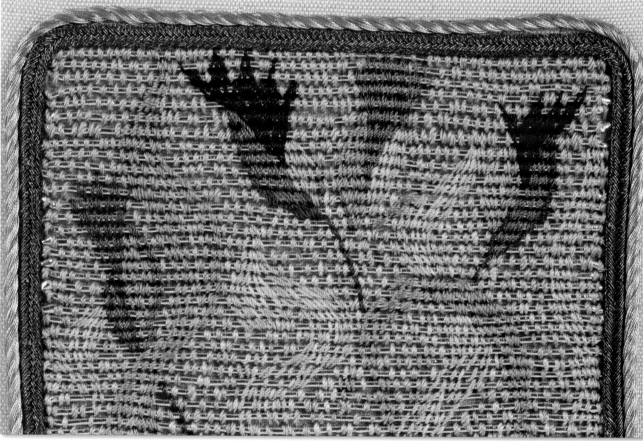

IDOL'S DRESS

TECHNIQUE: metal thread embroidery
DATE: late 18th century
PLACE OF ORIGIN: Spain
SIZE: 29 x 35cm (11½ x 13¾in)

At first glance, this appears to be a child's dress. Imagine having to wear it — how could it be washed? It is silk with a very heavy floral design in metal thread, couched and twisted. There is gold purl and spangles and a border trim of metallic lace.

In the 18th century, complex metal thread embroidery was made in professional workshops, where embroiderers spent many years as apprentices. A lot of metal thread work had an ecclesiastical purpose and this is a dress made for a religious image in a church or cathedral. Metallic lace is made from metal threads such as gold, silver or copper. Lace made from gold wire has been found in Egyptian tombs. Much later, France became renowned for gold lace production. From the 15th century onwards, metal lace was a combination of metal and textile threads.

Gifted by: Miss K. Paget
Embroiderers' Guild number: EG2585

Front of dress

Reverse of dress

CHINESE SLEEVE BANDS

TECHNIQUE: metal thread embroidery

DATE: 20th century

PLACE OF ORIGIN: China

SIZE: 92.5 x 9cm (36½ x 3½in)

Sleeve bands were designed to be attached to beautifully embroidered Chinese robes. This pair of sleeve bands feature metal thread. They have a cream satin background with a fretwork design in couched metal thread and roundels of flowers in silk thread. The flowers are peonies, which are regarded as the queen of flowers, standing for wealth and distinction. They are stitched in satin stitch shading – combinations of long and short straight stitch, which creates a shaded, slightly raised effect.

This pair of sleeve bands is interesting as it has a shop label attached to the back – 'Derry and Toms, Kensington' – a shop I remember well. The sleeve bands would have been made for the European market, but the designs are typically Chinese. Chinese embroidery was exported as early as the 13th century and by the 19th century, the city of Canton was an important centre for the export of textiles to Europe.

Gifted by: Miss Hester Clough
Embroiderers' Guild number: EG1987.86

STOMACHER

TECHNIQUE: hand embroidery; silk and metal thread
DATE: mid 18th century
PLACE OF ORIGIN: Great Britain
SIZE: 34 x 25cm (13³/₈ x 9¾in)

This is a stomacher, worn by grand ladies at court. It was worn as part of a gown on the front of the body, stiffened by a length of horn in the centre. It is designed to be seen and appreciated, as gowns were open-fronted in those days.

The fabric is fine linen, embroidered with floss silk threads. Gold threads are couched in circles and leaves and little white flowers are in long and short stitch. Notice the meandering vermicelli-style background threads. This is a quilting technique still used today, but it is now usually achieved using a sewing machine.

Gifted by: Lady Adam Gordon
Embroiderers' Guild number: EG1981.24

ROBE ADORNMENT

TECHNIQUE: hand embroidery; metal thread

DATE: 19th century

PLACE OF ORIGIN: India

SIZE: largest piece is 58 x 29cm (23 x 11½in)

These gorgeous pieces of embroidery from India would have adorned magnificent robes for ceremonial occasions. There is a yoke to be worn at the neck of the robe, sleeve panels and pocket trims.

The fabric is black silk, backed with red cotton and the embroidery is worked through both fabrics. The gold and silver metal threads are manipulated and couched down with orange thread, to form a geometric design of stylised flowers and leaves.

Gifted by: Sister Mary Magdalene

Embroiderers' Guild number: EG5123

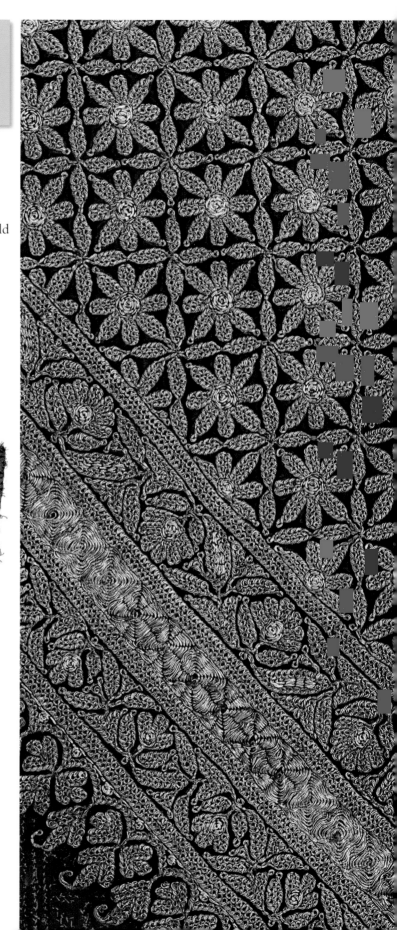

FLOWER PANEL

TECHNIQUE: silk embroidery with metal thread

DATE: 17th century

PLACE OF ORIGIN: Portugal

SIZE: 58 x 19cm (22¾ x 7½in)

This panel of cream silk brocade is stitched with silk and metal thread and mounted on a modern, synthetic fabric. Some areas have been padded. The stitches used are basket stitch, long and short stitch, French knots and couched gold thread.

This is a flower with attitude. It is meant to be seen from a distance. It is probably an example of ecclesiastical embroidery and might have been a panel from an altar frontal.

Gifted by: Lady Currie

Embroiderers' Guild number: EG4792

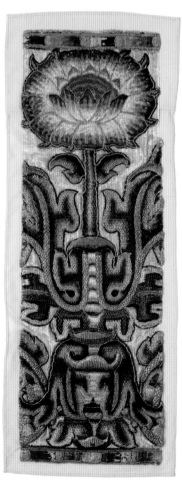

EMBROIDERED COVER

TECHNIQUE: metal thread

DATE: late 19th century

PLACE OF ORIGIN: India

SIZE: 114 x 61cm (44$^7/_8$ x 24in)

Indian embroideries are very diverse; from fine tambour work, where the embroidery is worked with a special hooked tool to create the appearance of chain stitch, through shisha mirrors and striking hand embroidery, to magnificent metal thread embellished with beads and embroidery in silk threads.

The embroidery on this cover is in the form of a border, embroidered on bright pink satin with couched metal threads and purls. Purl threads are fine metal strips wound like tiny springs, so they are very flexible. They can be stitched down in lengths or cut up to make tiny beads, which are then stitched in place. There are also metal sequins on this floral border. Silk thread has been used for the embroidery.

Embroiderers' Guild number: EG230

SCARF WITH REVERSIBLE EMBROIDERY

TECHNIQUE: hand embroidery; silk and metal thread

DATE: late 19th century (1877)

PLACE OF ORIGIN: Constantinople (Turkey)

SIZE: 252 x 54cm (99¼ x 21¼in)

This scarf or stole with its delicate floral design is astounding as it is completely reversible. Both sides appear identical. It is made of cotton organdie, stitched with silk threads and fine, gold metal thread.

Scarves such as this one were made in professional workshops, in designs that were thought to appeal to the Western market and were made specifically for the tourist trade or for export. Scarves similar to this one would have been for sale in the local bazaars. It is one of the donations gratefully received from Queen Mary in the early days of the Embroiderers' Guild.

Gifted by: HM Queen Mary
Embroiderers' Guild number: EG5024

STITCHES AND
MORE STITCHES

Atiny proportion of the stitches and techniques to be found in the Embroiderers' Guild Collection are covered in this chapter.

Tambour chain stitch embroidery is unusual because it is not worked with a needle, but with a fine hook and is worked from the back of the fabric. Similarly, shadow work is worked from the reverse of the fabric and the finished work, when viewed from the front, gives a shadowy effect of stitches behind.

We compare French and Pekin knots and look at plush stitch, one of the more complex stitches found in Berlin wool work.

COLLAR IN CHENILLE THREAD

TECHNIQUE: hand embroidery; chenille thread

DATE: 19th century

PLACE OF ORIGIN: Great Britain

SIZE: 95 x 18cm (37½ x 7in)

Here we have a third collar panel from the Collection. Compare it to the quirky fish scale embroidery and delicate straw work shown earlier (see pages 60 and 61). The chenille thread makes the flowers look extraordinarily rich and also realistic – we can see morning glories (ipomoea), carnations and daffodils.

The collar is stitched entirely in chenille threads, which are thick threads made of silk. The threads are couched to the background fabric by tiny stitches in silk thread, matching the colour of the chenille threads. Finer chenille threads could be stitched directly through the fabric with a large-eyed needle called a chenille needle. These are still used today. The background fabric of this collar is a black satin, which helps to emphasise the colour and richness of the flowers. There was once a delicate lace border, sadly now mostly worn away.

Gifted by: Mrs Guess in 1964
Embroiderers' Guild number: EG2007

3D CLEMATIS FLOWERS

TECHNIQUE: contemporary 3D needle lace
DATE: 21st century (2014)
PLACE OF ORIGIN: Great Britain
SIZE: 31 x 24cm (12¼ x 9½in)

This absolutely beautiful and inspiring example of contemporary needle lace, often known as raised embroidery, features clematis flowers, leaves and stems.

The background is painted and embroidered with a second layer in the form of slips, which are stitched separately and then applied to the background.

Maker: Kay Dennis
Kay is an internationally known embroiderer, tutor and author who specialises in stump work embroidery. Kay made this piece specially for this book.
Gifted by: Kay Dennis in 2014
Embroiderers' Guild number: not yet accessioned

SHADOW WORK MATS

TECHNIQUE: shadow work

DATE: 20th century (1957)

PLACE OF ORIGIN: Great Britain

SIZE: (large mat) 37.5 x 24.5cm (14¾ x 9¾in); (small mats) 16 x 17cm (6¼ x 6¾in)

These three charming mats with a design of flowers are a lady's dressing table set. The mats are worked on muslin so that the herringbone stitches show through, creating a shadow effect. Shadow embroidery is worked from the back of the fabric. Lightweight sheer fabrics are used so that a shadow effect is created on the right side. The thread used is silk and as well as herringbone stitch, chain stitch and backstitch have been used for outlines and as feature stitches to enhance the shadow effect.

They were made especially for the Needlework Development Scheme and that is why the mats are in excellent condition, as they have never been used. These mats are hand embroidered, but there are similarities in design with the machine-embroidered flower panels and tea cosy seen later in this book (see pages 102 and 103). The flowers on the large mat are strawberry and cherry flowers, but notice how the fruits are represented – just a few lines for the strawberries and cherries, but they are instantly recognisable.

Maker: Patricia Rooke

Gifted by: Needlework Development Scheme in 1962

Embroiderers' Guild numbers: (top) EG886; (bottom) EG886a; (middle) EG886b

These mats are on indefinite loan to the University of Edinburgh.

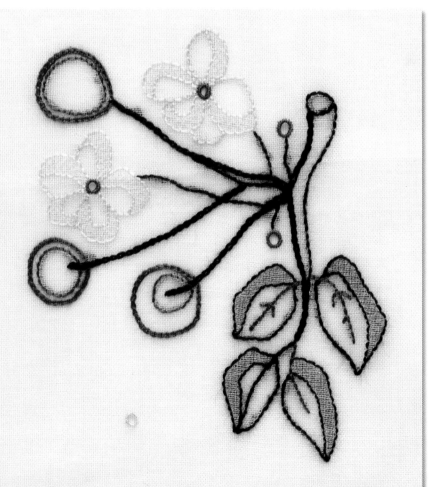

FRENCH KNOT FLOWERS

TECHNIQUE: hand embroidery; French knots

DATE: early 20th century

PLACE OF ORIGIN: Great Britain

SIZE: 35 x 29cm (13¾ x 11½in)

This panel is very skilfully made. The design of a vase of flowers is entirely filled with French knots. On page 84 there is an example of Pekin knots from China. Both knots are made by wrapping thread round a needle, but with French knots, the thread is wrapped round the needle several times. The design of the vase of flowers is formal and the colours are muted. The fabric and threads used are both cotton.

Maker: Miss Foster
Gifted by: Miss Foster
Embroiderers' Guild number: EG2693

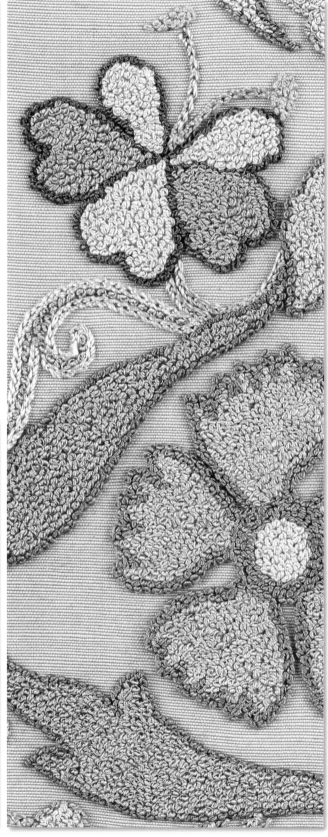

PEKIN KNOT SLEEVE BANDS

TECHNIQUE: Pekin knots

DATE: 19ᵗʰ century

PLACE OF ORIGIN: China

SIZE: 47 x 16.5cm (18½ x 6½in)

This pair of sleeve bands is joined together, all ready to be attached to an elaborate Chinese robe. The fabric and threads are silk and the beautiful rose, wisteria and daisies are set off by the couched gold threads surrounding them.

The technique to look out for here are the Pekin knots on the petals of the roses. This is similar to a French knot, but made in a slightly different way. In this stitch, thread is wrapped only once round the needle. It is known as the 'forbidden stitch' because when designs were filled in with rows of these tiny stitches, eye strain and even blindness could result. However, in China the Emperor's Palace is known as the Forbidden City and perhaps the term 'Forbidden stitch' comes from this, rather than the stitch being forbidden because of its association with blindness. The stitch can be worked in two ways. In one, it forms a tight knot and in the other, a tiny loop is made.

Embroiderers' Guild number: EG326

BERLIN WORK SHOWING PLUSH STITCH

TECHNIQUE: Berlin work; plush stitch
DATE: 19th century (1850)
PLACE OF ORIGIN: Great Britain
SIZE: 55 x 55cm (21¾ x 21¾in)

This is a very tactile panel, probably intended as a fire screen, and one of very few examples of plush stitch in the Embroiderers' Guild Collection.

Plush stitch is a very laborious technique where long loops of woollen thread are secured in a canvas fabric by cross stitches. Many loops are secured in this way. The loops are then cut and sculpted to form a dense, three-dimensional fabric. In this example, the roses are in plush stitch. The wool threads are aniline dyed and glass beads have been applied for additional shimmer.

This is an example of Berlin work, which was very popular in the 19th century. Designs in the form of coloured charts were produced, originally from Germany, and exported widely. Berlin wool thread on canvas was used to copy the charts exactly. The wool threads were chemically dyed and a huge range of bright, rich colours were available.

Embroiderers' Guild number: EG4134

ROCOCO STITCH

TECHNIQUE: rococo stitch
DATE: mid 17th century
PLACE OF ORIGIN: Great Britain
SIZE: 22 x 35.5cm (8½ x 14in)

This lovely and very rare piece from the 17th century is the only significant example of this stitch in the Collection. It was possibly designed to be a cushion cover and is embroidered on linen with silk threads.

The background is brick stitch and rococo stitch has been used for the flowers. Rococo stitch is also known as queen stitch and is a traditional canvas work stitch, dating from the 17th century. It is made using vertical stitches, which are crossed horizontally to produce a dense stitch. This design would have come from pattern books of designs that were available at this time. Roses, irises and carnations are featured.

Embroiderers' Guild number: EG807

TAMBOUR WORK

TECHNIQUE: tambour chain stitch embroidery

DATE: mid 18th century

PLACE OF ORIGIN: India (Gujarat)

SIZE: 91 x 88cm (35¾ x 34¾in)

I can only speculate as to the purpose of this fine embroidery, worked from the back using a tambour hook to produce a field of detailed flowers and stems. It is most probably part of the skirt of a dress.

These fabric designs, made in India, were popular in Europe for gowns and bed hangings and this piece would have been made for the European market. The woven cotton background is embroidered with silk thread. On the front of the fabric, the stitches resemble chain stitch. Tambour embroidery is often associated with beadwork, where the beads are strung on a thread and picked up individually as the hook is used to make a stitch. It is still used in the fashion industry today.

Gifted by: Lady Stokes

Embroiderers' Guild number: EG2324

SILK AND
WOOL

Silk, wool, linen, cotton and synthetics are the most popular fabrics used for embroidery and, in this chapter, we concentrate on silk and wool, which are both ancient in origin.

Spreading from Asia, silk is now universally used and it is arguably at its best in Chinese costume.

Whereas silk has associations with status and wealth, wool is evocative of warmth, comfort and practicality. The threads used are thicker, the colours more pronounced and embroideries stitched on or with wool are very different from their silken counterparts.

KIMONO COLLAR FRAGMENT

TECHNIQUE: hand embroidery; silk
DATE: early 20th century
PLACE OF ORIGIN: Japan
SIZE: 26 x 14cm (10¼ x 5½in)

This beautiful embroidery on silk fabric, silk threads and a little couched gold thread was meticulously stitched in Japan using satin stitch. It is a collar, to be worn inside a kimono to create a longer effect at the neck.

It originally belonged to a Japanese lady from Tokyo. We are lucky enough to have several pieces of Japanese embroidery in the Embroiderers' Guild Collection, but our pride and joy is an adult-sized kimono covered with gold motifs.

Gifted by: Jill Liddell, who was a well-respected traveller, collector, author and tutor of Japanese embroidery

Embroiderers' Guild number: EG1995.9

SILK PANEL

TECHNIQUE: hand embroidery; silk

DATE: 19th century

PLACE OF ORIGIN: China

SIZE: 40 x 26cm (15¾ x 10¼in)

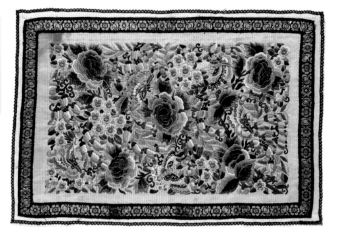

We have seen several examples of Chinese embroidery and silk embroidery from China forms a major part of the Embroiderers' Guild Collection. This beautiful panel is of yellow silk damask fabric decorated with flowers, leaves and butterflies.

It is hand stitched but with a machine-made, woven ribbon border, trimmed with braid. Fabric and threads are silk, in satin stitch, with a few tiny Pekin knots. The legs of the butterflies have been drawn in ink. It is not clear whether this was intentional, or whether the piece was not finished.

Embroiderers' Guild number: EG331

WOOL HANGING

TECHNIQUE: hand embroidery; wool

DATE: 20th century (1953)

PLACE OF ORIGIN: Great Britain

SIZE: 190 x 148cm (74¾ x 58¼in)

This large, dramatic hanging shows the expertise of Winsome Douglass' hand embroidery. The drama is increased by her limited colour palette of red, white and black. Her choice of fabric is red and white viyella with black woollen material. The design is of stylised flowers, birds, insects and animals in squares surrounding a large stylised flower.

Maker: Winsome Douglass

Winsome Douglass' life as a vibrant and talented artist and embroiderer has stretched back over 70 years. She made many pieces for the Needlework Development Scheme, but her speciality was toys, which are described as fabulous and glittering. Her books are much sought after.

Gifted by: Needlework Development Scheme in 1962

Embroiderers' Guild number: EG3927

WOOL POCKET

TECHNIQUE: wool embroidery on felt
DATE: 19th century
PLACE OF ORIGIN: Norway
SIZE: 21.5 x 15cm (8½ x 6in)

This little pocket comes from Norway and is one of the international pieces originally donated to the Needlework Development Scheme. I love the brightness of this piece and the way the design of flowers and leaves covers the background of red felt.

The thread is wool and the embroidery is in satin stitch. Sadly, we have no information as to the purpose of this pocket.

Gifted by: Needlework Development Scheme in 1962
Embroiderers' Guild number: EG2533
This pocket is on indefinite loan to Edinburgh University.

SILK DELPHINIUMS

TECHNIQUE: hand embroidery; silk
DATE: 20th century (1930)
PLACE OF ORIGIN: Great Britain
SIZE: 44.5 x 34cm (17½ x 13½cm)

This beautifully stitched and accurate representation of delphiniums sits in an oval frame and was stitched by Beryl Dean, a very talented embroiderer whose ecclesiastical work can be seen in many churches and cathedrals.

The background is satin and the threads are silk. It was stitched when Beryl was on a Royal School of Needlework Diploma course.

Maker: Beryl Dean
Gifted by: Beryl Dean
Embroiderers' Guild number: EG1991.15

SILK APRON

TECHNIQUE: hand embroidery

DATE: 19th century

PLACE OF ORIGIN: China

SIZE: 61 x 47cm (24 x 18½in)

This is another example of work made for the European market, rather than the country in which it was made. This apron panel was made in China. It is hand embroidered on black silk with silk threads, depicting a vase of flowers and a floral border – presumably thought to be a good design for the European market. The stitch used is simple straight stitch.

Embroiderers' Guild number: EG4523

CHINAI WORK

TECHNIQUE: hand embroidery

DATE: 20th century (1900–1950)

PLACE OF ORIGIN: India (Gujarat)

SIZE: (bottom) 40 x 6cm (15¾ x 2½in);
(top) 38 x 6cm (15 x 2½in)

Chinai (which means Chinese) work was done by Chinese immigrants to India from the 19th century and into the 20th century. There was a community of Chinese embroiderers who lived in Surat, South Gujarat. Their embroideries had Chinese characteristics of design and technique and were often narrow bands or borders of fine floss silk embroidery in a variety of stitches and often with floral designs.

The silk bands were particularly suited to the Indian market as they could be sewn onto saris or other garments and were very popular among the wealthy Parsee community. These two examples, both featuring rather stylised flowers, show straight stitch and Pekin knot stitch, the latter of which produces a rather knobbly texture. Pekin knots also feature in the Chinese piece on page 84.

Maker: Chinese immigrant workers, Surat, Gujarat in India

Gifted by: Mrs A. M. Johnstone

Embroiderers' Guild numbers: (top) EG3123; (bottom EG4379)

SILK CUSHION COVER

TECHNIQUE: hand embroidery

DATE: late 17th century

PLACE OF ORIGIN: Great Britain

SIZE: 27 x 26.5cm (10½ x 10¼in)

This beautiful cushion cover, made in the 17th century, features strawberries, violas and marigolds growing on a field of green silk, with a decorative tassel at each corner.

The threads are silk and the designs typical of floral designs from the 17th century that would have been available from pattern books and herbals. These could be readily purchased and often contained drawings of plants that had medicinal properties.

Gifted by: Miss Hester Clough

Embroiderers' Guild number: EG1987.104

MADE BY
MACHINE

Machine embroidery originated in the 19th century when mill owners were keen to develop methods that would speed up the production of textiles by their workers.

In the early 20th century, Dorothy Benson, working for the Singer Sewing Machine company, became a leading exponent of artistic machine embroidery, followed by others including Christine Risley and Joy Clucas.

Later and into the 21st century, machine embroidery has made a major impact in the embroidery world, although it is still not considered by some to be 'proper embroidery'.

WILD ROSE & SUNFLOWERS PANELS

TECHNIQUE: machine embroidery
DATE: 20th century (1966)
PLACE OF ORIGIN: Great Britain
SIZE: (far right) 16 x 24cm (6¼ x 9½in);
(right) 28.5 x 41cm (11¼ x 16in)

These pieces are called Wild Rose and Sunflowers. They were made by Joy Clucas, a significant machine embroiderer in the mid 20th century. Joy always embroidered her signature on her work, which is unusual among embroiderers.

The stitching is free machine embroidery, which means she used her machine with the feed dogs down. This technique allows the embroiderer to move her fabric freely, using the needle to draw her design.

The fabric and threads used here are cotton. Once again, the flowers are stylised, although yellow thread helps to identify the sunflowers, and the artist is entitled to put her own interpretation on her design.

Maker: Joy Clucas
Embroiderers' Guild numbers: (above right) EG2580; (above left) EG2691

100

TEA COSY

TECHNIQUE: machine embroidery

DATE: 20th century (1946)

PLACE OF ORIGIN: Great Britain

SIZE: 26 x 33cm (10¼ x 13in)

Another tea cosy and this one stitched in the year I was born. It is embroidered with silk thread on organdie fabric. A stitched label attached to the inside has the name Dorothy Benson and the information that it was stitched on a domestic sewing machine without the benefit of a motor or swing needle. This means that the machine was operated by a drive belt attached to a foot-operated treadle and could only stitch in straight lines.

The designer of the tea cosy was Frances Beal and the embroiderer was Dorothy Benson. Dorothy started work at the Singer Sewing Machine Company when she was only 14 and became head of the embroidery department. In this capacity she often embroidered the designs of others, including Rebecca Crompton, another well-known embroiderer of the time.

Dorothy Benson is considered to be the leading exponent of early machine embroidery and was the author of several books on the subject. She was a founder member of the Dorking branch of the Embroiderers' Guild and members today remember her as a quiet person, often to be found in charge of the coffee.

Maker: Dorothy Benson
Gifted by: Needlework Development Scheme in 1962
Embroiderers' Guild number: EG1035

WHITE TULIPS

TECHNIQUE: hand and
machine embroidery
DATE: 21st century (2010)
PLACE OF ORIGIN: Great Britain
SIZE: 108 x 48cm (42½ x 19in)

Maker: Audrey Walker
Purchased for the Embroiderers' Guild
Collection in 2011
Embroiderers' Guild number:
EG2012.6

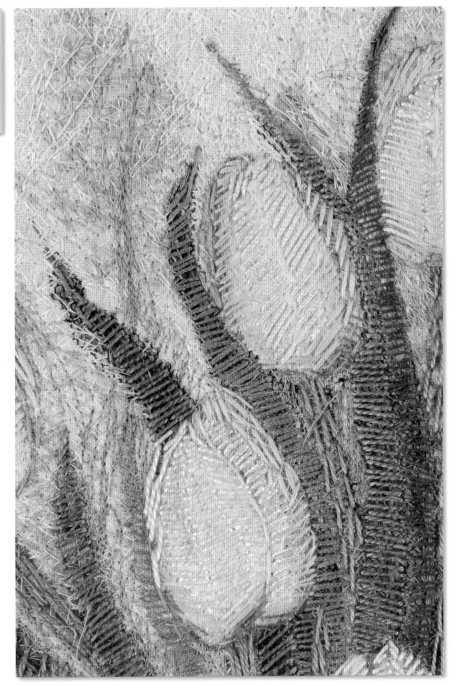

This is one of my favourite contemporary pieces, which should be described as textile art rather than embroidery. Since the 1980s, artists have been using many different techniques to create their textile art and here, machine and hand embroidery are used together.

The panel is stitched on craft Vilene with cotton machine threads and cotton perle for the hand embroidery. The panel is very calming, using a limited colour palette and dashes of shimmery threads. It is a panel designed to be hung on a wall – it looks good at a distance and also close up, when the stitches can be fully appreciated.

DOG ROSES

TECHNIQUE: machine-embroidered appliqué

DATE: 20th century (1980)

PLACE OF ORIGIN: Great Britain

SIZE: 98 x 69cm (38½ x 27¼in)

This fantastic example of textile art uses a technique that can be achieved quite easily using scraps of many different fabrics and colours, which are applied to a background and machine stitched in place using free machine embroidery.

The design is enhanced by some hand stitching in wool threads. Compare it to the White Tulips on page 103. This piece is worked very freely compared to the more structured tulips. The dog roses have great appeal from a distance. This piece is designed to hang on a wall. It is a wonderful example of how your imagination can really take hold when you have a pile of fabric scraps and a sewing machine set for freestyle embroidery.

Maker: Richard Box (textile artist, tutor, author and supporter of the Embroiderers' Guild)

Purchased for the Embroiderers' Guild Collection in 1983

Embroiderers' Guild number: EG1984.17

WHITEWORK HANDKERCHIEF

TECHNIQUE: whitework

DATE: late 19th century

PLACE OF ORIGIN: Switzerland

SIZE: 43 x 42cm (17 x 16½in)

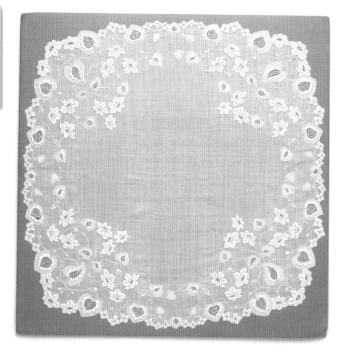

This exquisite whitework handkerchief was commercially made by machine, according to our catalogue. Swiss whitework, especially from St Gallen in Switzerland, was a cheaper, machine-made version of Ayrshire work, which this handkerchief resembles.

Ayrshire work originated in Scotland and spread throughout Europe. The style was similar to this handkerchief, with satin stitch and fine lace filling stitches on fine muslin. It was very popular for christening robes. The embroiderers were called 'Flowerers' because the intricate designs usually included flowers.

Gifted by: Miss H. E. Ionides, a donor of many embroideries to our Collection

Embroiderers' Guild number: EG424

SYMMETRY
IN STITCHES

The term symmetry means a design in which each half is a mirror image of the other. This is not true of all the pieces in this chapter, but they do represent repetitions of patterns. Borders of tablecloths where the design is repeated come under this category, and an Indian stole where the design is repeated at either end. Some designs, such as Evelyn Quainton's cushion cover (page 115) and Rachel Evans' mats (page 109), are truly symmetrical, as is the arrangement of bright red flowers on the piece from Turkey (page 108).

TURKISH TROUSER FRAGMENT

TECHNIQUE: hand embroidery

DATE: 19th century

PLACE OF ORIGIN: Turkey

SIZE: 59 x 37cm (23¼ x 14½in)

This fragment is hand stitched on cotton fabric and might have been part of a trouser leg. It is Turkish in style, but might have come from the Greek islands, as Greek and Turkish embroidery are very similar. Covered with a riot of red flowers, the fragment is stitched using straight stitch, with bright silk threads.

Gifted by: Mrs Essie Newberry (1878-1953)

Essie married the leading Egyptologist, Percy Newberry, and shared his interest in textiles. They collected textiles together from many parts of the World. Essie was a Vice President of the Embroiderers' Guild in 1922-1945 and honorary treasurer in 1935-1938. The Newberrys' extensive textile collection can be seen at the Ashmolean Museum, Oxford and the Whitworth Art Gallery, Manchester, with a few pieces donated to the Embroiderers' Guild.

Embroiderers' Guild number: EG4699

SYMMETRICAL DESIGNS

TECHNIQUE: hand embroidery

DATE: 20th century (1923)

PLACE OF ORIGIN: Great Britain

SIZE: (top) 18 x 18cm (7 x 7in);
(bottom) 16.5 x 16.5cm (6½ x 6½in)

These little panels are the work of another talented embroiderer about whom we know very little. These are original designs in traditional styles, influenced by the Arts and Crafts movement, led by William Morris.

Silk threads have been used on linen backgrounds with stem stitch, open chain and chain stitch, satin stitch, long and short stitch and brick stitch, with pattern darning and laid threads. Compare the stylised flowers of the lower piece with the more realistic flowers on the top piece. These are pomegranates, which are of course fruits, but there are tiny blue forget-me-nots in the background. Notice the detailed stitching of the background of this piece.

Maker: Miss Rachel K. Evans
Gifted by: Miss Rachel K. Evans
Embroiderers' Guild numbers: (top) EG2681; (bottom) EG1982.67

HANDKERCHIEF SACHET

TECHNIQUE: hand embroidery

DATE: 20th century

PLACE OF ORIGIN: Great Britain

SIZE: 20 x 20cm (8 x 8in)

This is a handkerchief sachet in a traditional floral design of daisies, tulips and bluebells. The fabric is linen, the threads are silk and it has been worked in straight stitch. Each side has a different design (see below, left). This piece and the work of Rachel K. Evans on page 109 exemplify to me what embroidery is all about.

Maker: Joan H. Drew (1875–1961)

Joan lived in Surrey and was much involved with the Women's Institute. She was a self-taught embroiderer, becoming a teacher herself, especially of children. She is famous for her banners and wall hangings.

Gifted by: Miss Kathleen Aldworth

Embroiderers' Guild number: EG4781

SASH FRAGMENT

TECHNIQUE: hand embroidery

DATE: 19th century

PLACE OF ORIGIN: Greece

SIZE: 21 x 18.5cm (8¼ x 7¼in)

Embroidery from Greece and Turkey plays an important part in the Embroiderers' Guild Collection as our first president, Louisa Pesel, and her friend Essie Newberry were experts in the field and donated pieces for inspiration and study in the early days of the Guild.

This piece is probably a fragment of a sash; the embroidery is faded and worn, but painstakingly executed and these fragments are reminders of a gentler way of life in a faraway land. The fabric is linen and the floral sprays are stitched with silk threads.

Gifted by: Mrs Essie Newberry (1878-1953)
Embroiderers' Guild number: EG3640

KASHMIR SHAWL

TECHNIQUE: hand embroidery

DATE: mid 19th century

PLACE OF ORIGIN: India (Kashmir)

SIZE: 240 x 50cm (94½ x 19¾in)

This sumptuously beautiful shawl was professionally embroidered in Delhi on black and green woollen shawl cloths from Kashmir. The green panels have been inserted into the main black cloth.

The threads are floss silk in vibrant colours using satin, stem, long and short and straight stitch. I love the softness of the Kashmir shawl cloth. The design features the buta or boteh, which is a droplet-shaped design that originally came from Persia – also now known as the Paisley design.

Embroiderers' Guild number: EG4474

TABLECLOTH

TECHNIQUE: hand embroidery; tambour embroidery and torchon lace

DATE: 19th century

PLACE OF ORIGIN: India

SIZE: 91 x 91cm (35¾ x 35¾in)

This tablecloth is worked entirely in yellow silk thread, to stunning effect. The technique is tambour work, which we saw earlier in the book (see pages 76 and 87).

This example is less finely done and was probably also made for the European market. The torchon lace border adds a further touch of luxury.

Embroiderers' Guild number: EG5848

VELVET CUSHION COVER

TECHNIQUE: hand embroidery on velvet
DATE: 20th century (1910)
PLACE OF ORIGIN: Great Britain
SIZE: 45cm (17¾in) in diameter

This cushion cover front would make a very comfortable cushion, stitched as it is, in perle threads on soft velvet fabric.

This is an original design of primroses and cowslips stitched using straight stitch, with tiny French knots in the background, stitched in a finer thread. I see this cushion in a country cottage on a chair by a roaring fire. It is another of my favourite pieces.

Maker: Eveline Quainton
This embroiderer trained at Putney School of Art from 1910–1912. She went on to work in a large workroom, making lampshades and parasols. It was a very exclusive business.
Gifted by: Miss Phyllis Roberts, who was Eveline's cousin
Embroiderers' Guild number: EG1984.18

BORDER TABLECLOTH

TECHNIQUE: hand embroidery

DATE: 20th century (1912)

PLACE OF ORIGIN: Great Britain

SIZE: 105 x 100cm (41¼ x 39¼in)

This beautiful tablecloth, with very fine detail, was designed to be used and laundered. It is a wonderful example of embroidery, so fine you wonder how it could be achieved by hand.

The flowers form a border round the edge of the cloth. This would look wonderful today on a table with a bone china tea set and plate of cakes.

Maker: designed and made by Mrs Kathleen M. Harris (1880-1963)

Kathleen was a lecturer and teacher of embroidery who led the first embroidery course for the Embroiderers' Guild and was editor of *Embroidery* magazine from 1951-1960, which is still published today. On her retirement, she became president of the Sussex branch of the Embroiderers' Guild.

Gifted by: Mrs Kathleen M. Harris

Embroiderers' Guild number: EG2718

TEA COSY

TECHNIQUE: hand embroidery

DATE: 20th century (1910–1919)

PLACE OF ORIGIN: Great Britain

SIZE: 26 x 33cm (10¼ x 13in)

I love the way the design of this tea cosy covers the whole of the front. The design, of yellow poppies on white linen and with twisted silk threads, features chain stitch, herringbone, long and short stitch, buttonhole stitch, feather and fly stitch.

The cosy is an art needlework design. This was surface embroidery, popular in the late 19th and early 20th centuries. It was influenced by the Arts and Crafts Movement, led by William Morris. The freestyle designs were very different from the Berlin wool work designs, in bright colours and which were stitched from charts. Berlin work can be seen in the tea cosy on page 25, for example. The flowers here are very realistic and expertly embroidered.

Maker: Elsie Marianne Grimes

Elsie was a descendant of Cecil Aldin, the painter and Illustrator.

Gifted by: This tea cosy was rescued from a jumble sale in 1983 and donated to the Embroiderers' Guild by Bridget Moss.

Embroiderers' Guild number: EG1983.154

IRREGULAR DESIGNS

This final chapter is for beautiful embroidery that does not easily fit into another category. Some are indeed irregular designs with no repeat patterns, but most have interesting stories behind them, such as the hot iron transfers, often despised by today's textile artists, but once the mainstay of embroiderers everywhere.

It also features work by schoolchildren before they became well-respected embroiderers, and others with an interesting history.

EMBROIDERED POCKET

TECHNIQUE: hand embroidery

DATE: early 18th century

PLACE OF ORIGIN: Great Britain

SIZE: 33 x 30cm (13 x 11¾in)

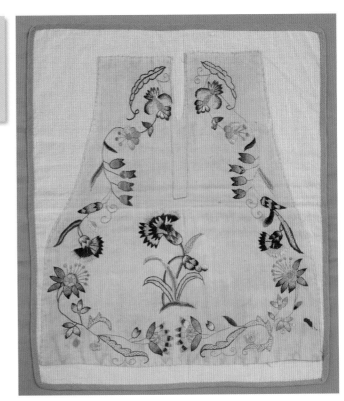

In the 18th century, pockets for women were not part of clothes as they are today, but were separate pieces worn under their petticoats. There were usually ties that fastened round the waist and the pocket could be reached by an opening in the seam of the petticoat. Pockets were worn as pairs and were the handbags of the day.

Interestingly, men's pockets of the time were sewn into garments much as they are today. This pocket is hand embroidered on linen using long and short stitch. The red flowers are clearly carnations.

Embroiderers' Guild number: EG1601

FRAMED BUTTERCUPS

TECHNIQUE: hand embroidery
DATE: 20th century (1910)
PLACE OF ORIGIN: Great Britain
SIZE: 29 x 37cm (11½ x 14½in)

Silk threads and needle lace add an extra dimension to this beautiful example of hand embroidery. It is a naturalistic design, depicting buttercups. The background is black fabric and the threads used are silk. Sadly, we have no information about the maker.

Embroiderers' Guild number: EG1990.28

HOT IRON TRANSFER PANEL

TECHNIQUE: hand embroidery from a transfer design
DATE: 20th century (1950s)
PLACE OF ORIGIN: Great Britain
SIZE: 60 x 52in (23½ x 20½in)

This is such an exuberant bouquet of flowers. Furnishing fabric has been used for the background of this panel and the thread is stranded cotton. The design is typical of hot iron transfer designs of the 1950s.

Hot iron transfers were a popular method of transferring a design to fabric. The paper transfer was laid in position on the fabric and ironed until the design appeared on the fabric. Transfers were published in magazines and the Embroiderers' Guild published their own transfer designs, which were very popular. Sadly, they are no longer available.

This panel was donated to an Embroiderers' Guild fundraising auction in 2008, which was held in association with the Knitting and Stitching Shows.

Maker: Nancy Olive Bryson
Nancy was a teacher and embroiderer of distinction who lived in Westcliff-on-Sea in Essex, UK.
Gifted by: Maureen Bryson, who was Nancy's daughter-in-law
Embroiderers' Guild number: not yet accessioned

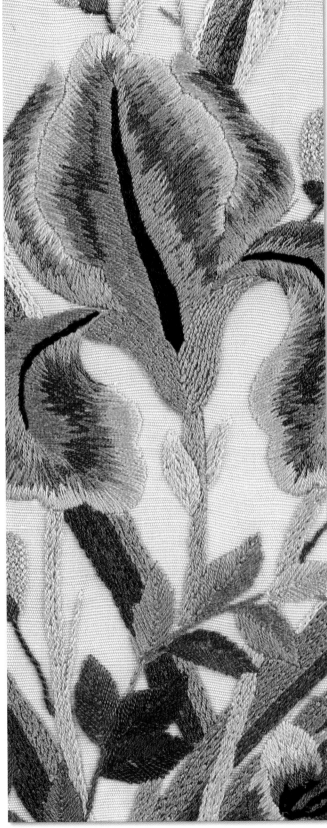

ELIZABETHAN-STYLE BAG

TECHNIQUE: hand embroidery

DATE: 20th century (1915)

PLACE OF ORIGIN: Great Britain

SIZE: 19 x 12cm (7½ x 4¾in)

This bag was made in the style of an Elizabethan bag and represents another example of outstanding hand embroidery. Using a variety of hand embroidered stitches in silk thread, this bag was originally on loan to the Embroiderers' Guild Collection, but was purchased in 2003.

Maker: Elsie Myrtle Williams
Purchased from: Mrs Elizabeth Mace
Embroiderers' Guild number: EG2006.12

WILDFLOWERS PANEL

TECHNIQUE: hand embroidery

DATE: 20th century (1923)

PLACE OF ORIGIN: Great Britain

SIZE: 46 x 28cm (18 x 11in)

This lovely piece is reminiscent of a field of wild flowers in summer. It is stitched on linen using wool threads. The stitches used are stem stitch, chain, straight and buttonhole stitch, bullion knots and seeding. Bullion knots are made in a similar way to French knots, but long needles are used and the thread is wrapped round the needle many times to create a sausage shape. This piece has the freedom of embroidery that we find in our young embroiderers of today.

Maker: Mrs Nancy Stanfield, while she was a student at Cheltenham Ladies College

Gifted by: Mrs Nancy Stanfield

Embroiderers' Guild number: EG1983.159

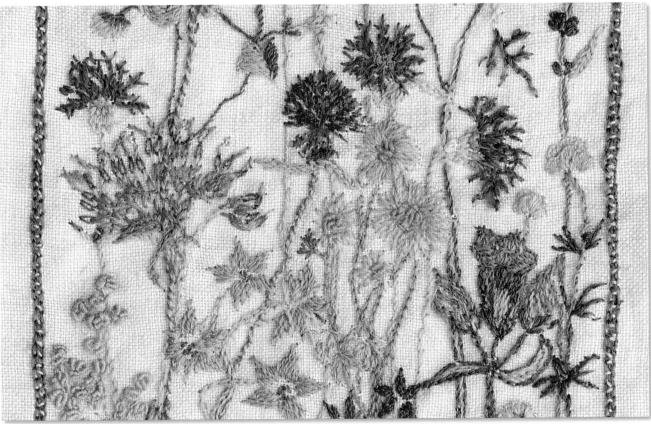

CARNATION PANEL

TECHNIQUE: hand embroidery
DATE: 18th century
PLACE OF ORIGIN: Greece (Samos, Aegean Islands)
SIZE: 119 x 48.5cm (46¾ x 19in)

These bright colours from a sunny climate show exuberant flowers in silk threads on a linen background. This is a long panel with large, carnation-like flowers along the length.

Gifted by: Lady Olga Egerton
Embroiderers' Guild number: EG216

FIRESCREEN PANEL

TECHNIQUE: hand embroidery using hot iron transfer
DATE: 20th century (1951)
PLACE OF ORIGIN: Great Britain
SIZE: 61 x 41.5cm (24 x 16¼in)

This panel is likely to have been made as a firescreen. The design was printed onto the cotton fabric using a hot iron transfer. The threads are stranded cotton and the stitches used are mainly satin and stem stitches with a grid of straight stitches, and cross stitches at the intersections of the grid, on the vase.

The flowers in this exuberant design are quite recognisable, with morning glories, roses, hollyhocks, narcissi, carnations, tulips and others. Unusually, the embroiderer has signed her work in stitching: M. L. Ellis, 1951.

Among the riot of colourful flowers is an equally colourful bird, not recognisable as a British bird but a hint as to what will be found in the next book in this series, *Embroidered Treasures: Birds*.

Maker: M. L. Ellis
Embroiderers' Guild number: not yet accessioned

126